CHILDREN'S *PSALMS
to pray, sing & do

DAVID HASS

ILLUSTRATIONS BY BRENT BECK

ST. ANTHONY MESSENGER PRESS

Cincinnati, Ohio

Cover and book design by Mark Sullivan
Illustrations by Brent Beck

Library of Congress Cataloging-in-Publication Data

Haas, David.
  Children's psalms to pray, sing, and do / by David Haas.
      p. cm.
  Summary: A topically arranged collection of psalms accompanied by prayers,
activities, and reflection questions.
  ISBN 0-86716-453-0 (alk. paper)
  1. Bible stories, English—O.T. Psalms. [1. Bible. O.T. Psalms.] I.
Title.
  BS1430.5H37 2003
  223'.209505—dc22
                              2003022206

ISBN 0-86716-453-0

Table of Contents

A Letter to You from Me

A Letter to You from Me

Dear children,

This is a book of prayers that were originally written a long time ago.

They come from the Bible, and they are called "Psalms."
These prayers, while very old, still have a message for us today.
They are wonderful gifts from God, and they are meant for all of us.
They are for you, too.

God knows absolutely everything that goes on in our lives, and because of that, God gives us help. God gives us the words in these prayers so we can truly express what we feel, no matter what those feelings might be: joy, sadness, excitement or worry. There is a prayer in this book somewhere that will help you say to God what is in your heart.

We need to remember that it is okay for us to feel whatever we feel.
God wants to hear from us, and cares what happens to us.
God always listens.
God always loves us.
God is always near.

Some of these prayers might sound familiar to you.
We sing these prayers when we go to Mass on Sunday, so
some of the words will sound the same.

You can sing these prayers.
You can say these prayers out loud or quietly.
You can pray them alone, with your family or in a group with your friends.

For me, the Psalms have always helped me in my life.
They have always been a wonderful way for me to talk to God,
and for God to speak to me.

I bet it will be the same with you.

Remember,
God is always listening, and is always waiting to hear from us.

David Haas

Psalms for when I am happy

Let me see your face shine!

God, let me see your
face shine!
When I call to you,
please listen to me,
because I know you are
the one
who will always take
care of me.
Please hear my prayer.

I know that God can do
wonderful things
if we are good and
faithful.
God always hears me,
always listens.

4

God, let your light
shine.
For when you do so,
our hearts are glad
and happy.

When I go to bed, I am
calm and peaceful,
because I know you
are with me
and you keep me safe.

God, let me see your
face shine!

*What are some of God's gifts? Are they flowers, the trees and
the sunshine? Do you have a close friend or a family member
that helps you see God's gifts? Sometimes we can see God's
face shine inside the people we love the most!*

Your words

God, your words
give us life.
God's law is the right law,
and it is perfect.
We can put our trust in
God's law,
for God's law takes
care of us.

God's rules are for our
good,
food for our heart.

What rules do you obey at home? Do you have to clean your room, do your homework or share your toys? What are some of the rules that God gives all of us to follow? How do these rules help make your life more happy?

give us life!

When we hear God's command,
things are easier for us.

We should always honor and pray to God,
for God has a good plan for all of us.

God's words are more wonderful than any gift,
better than gold, better than anything!
God, your words give us life.

"The law of the LORD is perfect, reviving the soul."
[PSALM 19]

7

I love you and praise you!

I love you and praise you, my God!
I love you and praise you
because you always help me.
You keep harmful people away from me.

We should always sing and dance to God,
so we will always remember
that God is special,
that God is holy.

"You have turned my mourning into dancing."
[P S A L M 30]

8

If God gets angry, the
anger goes away very
quickly,
because God loves us
so much.

God, I know you will
always help me.
When I am sad,
you dry my tears,
and I feel happier than
ever!

I love you and praise
you, my God!

What do you do when you feel sad, angry or upset? Do you cry? Do you yell? Do hurt someone else's feelings? Or do you pray to God and ask for help? Sometimes when we are angry or we are upset it helps to pray. God will help us to feel better. Try it sometime!

9

I will always

I will always bless God.
I will always bless God,
all the time!
I will sing out about how
awesome God is,
and everyone, especially
those who are sad,
will hear me, and they,
too, will be glad.

What songs do you know that bless and praise God? What is your favorite song that praises God? Think about all the wonderful things that God has done for you, and make that part of the song. Sing it out loud! Sing it in the bathtub! Sing it with your friends! Sing! Sing! Sing!

bless God!

Come with me,
everybody!
Come and sing about
God to everyone we
meet.
Whenever I pray and
look to God, God
answers me,
and helps me to be at
peace.

If you want to be happy,
God will help you.
With God you will never
feel bad about yourself.
Whenever poor people
call out to God,
God takes care of them.

"My soul makes its boast
in the LORD; let the humble
hear and be glad"
[PSALM 34]

Taste and see how good
God can be;
and we are blessed
and holy if we lean
on God.

I will always bless God.

11

How beautiful is your home

How beautiful
is your home, O God!
I want to be
with you, God!
More than anything, I
want to be with you!
My heart is pounding,
just thinking about
being with you.

If we are with you,
we are happy.
You make us strong.

"How lovely is your dwelling place, O LORD of hosts!"
[PSALM 84]

Hear us, God!
Please look down
upon us,
all of us whom you
have chosen.

How beautiful is your
home, O God!

Where do you go to seek God? At church? At home? In your yard? On the school bus? (Hint: No matter where you search, you'll find God. God is everywhere!)

13

Blessed are we

Blessed are we when we follow your commands.

Blessed are we when we follow you perfectly, when we follow your laws!

Blessed are we when we obey your commands, and seek you with all our heart.

What commandment of God do you follow that makes you happy? Do you try to listen to your parents and teachers, and follow their example and ways? I am sure that makes them happy, because they want what is best for you. Seeing happiness in others makes us happy, too!

14

Be good to us, that we
may always keep your
commands.
Open our eyes so that
we can see
the many wonders that
you create!

Teach me, God.
Teach me your ways.
Help me to choose well,
and keep your
commands
close to my heart.

Blessed are we when
we follow your
commands.

"Happy are those whose
way is blameless,
who walk in the law
of the LORD."
[PSALM 119]

when
we
follow
your
commands

We are the people of God

We are the people
of God.
Sing with joy, everyone!
Serve God, and be
happy about it!
Sing songs to God!

Remember that we have
a wonderful God,
and God made us.

"Worship the LORD with
gladness; come into his
presence singing."
[P S A L M 100]

We are the people
of God, and we are
taken care of.
God is so good. God is
always forgiving us,
never leaving us alone
and giving us
everything we need all
the time!

We are the people
of God.

*Take a few moments and think about all of the times when
God has taken care of you, or forgiven you, or been by your
side when you felt alone. In return, we are asked to serve each
other in the same way. How do you serve God? How does
God serve you?*

We will be

When you come again,
we will be so happy!
Shout and sing praise to
God!
God is so kind,
And we should always
sing praise!

How do you celebrate God's greatness? Do you sing out with
joy at church? Do you say your prayers each morning and at
night? Do you pray with your family before meals and thank
God for your food? Do you thank God for the rain, the clouds,
the grass on the hills?

so happy!

God gives us hope,
God heals our bodies,
God gives every star in
the sky a name!

God is so great and
powerful!
God understands
everything.
Come now!
Celebrate, sing, dance,
jump and shout!
Sing to God!
When you come again,
we will be so happy!

"He covers the heavens
with clouds, prepares rain
for the earth, makes grass
grow on the hills."
[PSALM 147]

19

We will be close to God!

"O LORD, who may abide in your tent? Who may dwell on your holy hill?"
[PSALM 15]

If we do what is right, we will be close to God.

If we always do what is right, if our lives are good, if we always speak the truth, and if we do not say bad things about other people, God will reward us.

We should never harm others, and never spread lies about people. We should always think the best things, and remember that God is holy.

We should never ask for more than what people can give.
We should never trick people into doing bad things.

If we do what is right, we will be close to God.

In Psalm 15 we are given some good instructions as to how we can be close to God forever. How are you doing? Look at Psalm 15 again, look closely at the list of things that God is asking us. Ask a parent or another adult to help you make a list of ways you can follow God's way every day.

How to make your list:
Use crayons or markers and make the words large enough for you to see and read from a distance. Hang the list where you can see it everyday before you leave for school or run out to play with friends. Here are some suggestions for your list: I will not harm another. I will not spread lies. I will not trick my friends. I will share my toys. I will not ask for things I know my family cannot afford. I will try to be holy like God is holy.

Psalms for when I want to thank and praise God!

Your name

God, your name is a wonderful name!
I look up to the sky that is
made by your hands and your heart.
I look up at the moon and stars
that you also made,
and I wonder:
What did we do to deserve these
wonderful things?
Why do you care for us?
Why do you love us so much?

*What are some of your favorite creations of God? Your family?
Your friends? Your pet? Animals at the zoo? Can you believe
that God thinks you are at the top of the list?*

is a wonderful name!

You make us feel that
we are so special.
You make us feel
wonderful and glorious!
You give us so many
living things:
all of the creatures,
the birds, the fish, and
everything that flies,
crawls and swims.

God, your name is a
wonderful name!

"You have put all things
under their feet, all sheep
and oxen, and also the
beasts of the field, the
birds of the air, and the
fish of the sea, whatever
passes along the paths
of the seas."
[PSALM 8]

25

It is so good to thank you

God, it is good to thank
you, always.
It is so good to
thank you,
and to sing about you
to everyone we meet!
You are so kind, so I
have to sing about it!
You are always there,
so I have to sing
about it!

"For you, O LORD, have
made me glad by your
work; at the works of your
hands I sing for joy."
[PSALM 92]

We will grow well, like trees,
like trees that are planted in God's house.
We will always bloom, even when we are old;
always filled with energy and joy!

We are strong and we will always sing,
sing about you God, who gives us this strength.

God, it is good to thank you, always.

What are you most grateful for: your family, your school, your friends? How do you thank God? Do you sing it? Pray it? Or do you tell everyone you meet how happy and thankful you are to be alive?

All good

God, all good things come
from you.
Your love is everywhere,
down here on earth,
and up to the heavens,
through the clouds!
How deep is your love!

What is the best gift that God has ever given you? How do you thank God for it?

things come from you

We are filled with your
love.
We can taste it.
We can feel it!

Yes God,
you give us everything
that is good.
You give us light in the
darkness.
Please, never stop
loving us!

God, all good things
come from you.

"For with you is the
fountain of life; in your
light we see light."
[PSALM 36]

God is in charge!

"Clap your hands, all you peoples; shout to God with loud songs of joy."
[PSALM 47]

Blow the horn loudly!
God is in charge!
Everyone should clap
his or her hands,
and sing and shout to
God!
God is the ruler of all!

God is higher than
anything else,
and the trumpets blow
loudly for God!
We hope that the music
will never stop,
so play and sing louder
and longer!

God is in charge of
everything,
so do your best!
God is the ruler of
heaven and earth.

God sits high,
but looks low,
and is in love with
everything!

Blow the horn loudly!
God is in charge!

What special talents, or gifts from God, do you have? Can you dance? Can you sing? Can you draw, paint, act, build, run fast or speak two languages? Maybe you are very funny and you can make everyone laugh? Maybe you are smart and you can read lots of books? We are all unique and we are all special. God gives us many talents and special gifts. We don't have to call God up on the phone, or look way up high into the heavens to find God. God is in all we do—up high or down low.

Sing

Sing Alleluia! Everyone!
Be joyful to God,
everywhere you look and
walk;
sing happy songs about
God!
Sing songs like:
"God you are so
wonderful, and you are
so awesome!"

Everyone should make up
songs of praise!

How do you tell people how great God is? Do you point out a pretty flower or sing a song about the glorious day? Do you smile at strangers on the street? There are just so many ways to say, smile or sing, "God, you are so awesome!" to everyone you meet!

Alleluia!

Everyone, come and see
how fantastic God is!

God made the sea into
ground,
so those who were on
their way to safety
could travel to a safe
place.

Listen now, everyone!
God has done wonderful
things for me,
so all of us should bless
and praise God,
for God is kind to us!

Sing Alleluia! Everyone!

"Say to God:
'How awesome are your
deeds!'"
[PSALM 66]

I want to sing!

I want to sing!
Help me to feel one
with you,
never far away.
You are so good. Please
rescue me
from all pain and
sadness.

God, I need you to be
my hero.
I need you to save me.
Keep me far away from
those
who want to hurt me.

"My lips will shout for joy
when I sing praises to
you; my soul also, which
you have rescued."
[PSALM 71]

You are the only one for me.
I have always trusted you, and
I have leaned on you since I
was born.
You knew me before I was born.

I will always sing about you,
and all of the fantastic things
you do.
You have always taught me,
and I have learned well.
I remember all of the good
things I have,
because of you.

I want to sing!

God is our hero. But, God also sends us heroes here on Earth to help us and protect us and to guide our way. Do you have a hero in your life? Who do you look up to the most: your mom, dad, grandmother or grandfather? Or is there someone else? What do you admire most about your hero? How do they help you to become a better person?

We shall

Everywhere we look,
we shall see God's
power!

Sing to God
a new song,
for we are blessed
with so many
wonderful things!
God is victorious!

*What are some of the ways you witness the power of God?
Remember, the power of God comes in many forms. It is the
drop of rain on a flower petal and it is the loud thunderclap
during a rainstorm too. It is the gentle touch of a warm hand
and it is the strong arms reaching out to save you. God's
power touches everything in many, many ways.*

see God's power!

God lets us see how
wonderful things
can be,
and never lets us down,
for God is always kind
and merciful to us.

All people,
all creatures
everywhere
see how wonderful
God is.
Keep singing wonderful
songs of praise to God!

Everywhere we look, we
shall see God's power!

"All the ends of the earth
have seen the victory of
our God."
[PSALM 98]

Alleluia!

"From the rising of the sun
to its setting the name
of the LORD is to be
praised."
[PSALM 113]

Alleluia! Alleluia!
You always help the
poor,
so we must praise you.
We must serve you,
and we should bless
you always!

God, you are high
above!
God, your glory is
beyond our sight!
God, no one is like you!
No other god would
look down from on high
and love us so well!

38

Alleluia!

You raise us up!
You help the poor!
You make us feel that
we are special,
grand and wonderful!

Alleluia! Alleluia!

What are some of the ways you can serve God? Do you try to spend time with other children you know who may be poor? Do you share? Do you try to be a friend to an older person?

This day

This day belongs to God!
Be happy! Be glad!
Everyone, give thanks to
our God!
God is a good God!
All the time!

The right hand of God is a
mighty hand,
filled with power!
I will never die,
because with God I can
live forever!

What are some ways you can show that you are happy to be alive today? Do you smile? Do you laugh? Do you clap your hands and sing? Do you jump up and down or dance around? There are just so many ways to say, "I am happy and I am glad God made this day for me!"

belongs to God!

God keeps us all steady
and safe,
and we are so happy
that God has done
these things!
We are seeing
wonderful things!

This day belongs
to God! Be happy!
Be glad!

"This is the day the LORD
has made; let us rejoice
and be glad in it."
[PSALM 118]

Let us enter God's house!

Let us sing and rejoice!
Let us enter God's
house!

I rejoice when people
say to me,
"Let's go to God's
house."
I am very near, close to
the door,
ready to greet you,
God.

Pray for peace,
pray for peace here and
everywhere!

"For the sake of my
relatives and friends
I will say, 'Peace be
within you.'"
[PSALM 122]

May all of us know
peace,
and may blessings be
with us always!

Because you are all my
family, and
because you are all my
friends,
I will say, "Peace be
with you."
I will always pray for
you.

Let us sing and rejoice!
Let us enter God's
house!

God wants to be close to you. God is your family and your friend, so try to take some time out to see God and wish God well. When we go to church on Sunday, we are at home with God in a special way. What do like most about that time on Sunday? Singing? Praying? Sharing the sign of peace with each other?

God is so

God is so wonderful
to us!

Every time God heals and
blesses us,
it is like a dream, so hard
to believe!
When we think about it,
we begin to laugh, sing
and rejoice!

Can you think of a time God healed or blessed you or someone you love? Was someone you loved sick or hurt or in the hospital? How did God heal or bless you? How did you thank God?

wonderful to us!

God is so wonderful,
and we are so happy!

Help us to always find
happiness, God.
For those who cry, will
soon be happy again.

God is so wonderful
to us!

"The LORD has done
great things for us,
and we rejoiced."
[PSALM 126]

Praise God!

"Let everything that breathes praise the LORD!"
[PSALM 150]

Praise God! Alleluia!

Praise God in all holy places!
Praise God in the heavens!
Praise God for awesome good things!
Praise God - God is great!

Sing Praise with trumpets and horns!
Sing Praise with guitars and harps!
Sing Praise with drums —loud drums!

46

Sing Praise—and dance,
dance, dance!

Shout Praise with
cymbals!
Shout Praise with
banging, clanging
cymbals!
Shout Praise with all
that you have!
Shout Praise with
everything you've got!

Praise God! Alleluia!

God loves to see creation dance and sing. In fact, some people say that singing is like praying twice! When we sing, God hears us and feels the vibrations of our happy music. Nothing delights God more! Sing out a joyful song. Ask an adult to put on some music! Together, dance and sing out loud so that God can hear your prayers—twice!

47

Psalms for when I need God

Why have you left me alone?

"O my God, I cry by day, but you do not answer; and by night, but find no rest."
[PSALM 22]

God, why have you left me alone?

Everyone makes fun of me,
they tease me, and
poke at me, saying:
"You think God will take care of you?
Ha! If God really loves you, let God come to you now!"

Sometimes I feel like I
am surrounded
by mean people.
They hurt me, and I can
feel the pain.

God, please come to
me now!
I need you. Come and
help me!

Do you ever feel alone or that no one is on your side? Do
children at school say mean or hurtful things? Sometimes do
you feel like no one understands you or listens to you? In
times like these, it is a comfort to know that all you have to
say is, "God, please come to me now! I need you." And God
will be there. God is always there for you, for all of us.

You are in

God, you are in charge of my life.

God, I look for you to feel safe, so please, never let me feel scared. Please come and help me, I want to feel safe in your hands.

There are people who want to harm me.

Do you feel lonely or afraid when you are by yourself and there is darkness all around? Praying to God when you're lonely or afraid is like getting a big hug from someone you love the most, like your mom or your dad or maybe your best friend. Remember, we are all God's children, and God is always there for us.

charge of my life

There are other people who forget me, and still others who make me feel awful.

I have to remember to put my trust in you.
You are my God,
you are in charge of my life,
and you will protect me from all that is hurtful.

Keep smiling on me, God,
Keep loving me.

God, you are in charge of my life.

"Be a rock of refuge for me, a strong fortress to save me."
[PSALM 31]

53

I need you to heal me

God, I need you
to heal me.

People are happy
when God
cares for them.
When bad things
happen,
God will be there.
God will guard
everyone
and give them good
things.
When we are sick,
God will take care
of us.

"Happy are those who
consider the poor; the
LORD delivers them in the
day of trouble."
[PSALM 41]

God, please heal me,
For I have sinned.
Other people want me
to feel bad,
and I do.
But I believe you can
help me
feel better about
myself.

God, I need you
to heal me.

When we lie to our friends or parents, hurt someone else's feelings with mean words, or cheat on a test, we hurt ourselves as well. These kinds of things hurt everyone. When you feel bad about our actions, how does God help you feel better? What makes you feel better? Do you say you are "sorry?" Do you try better to be kind? Do make an effort to consider other people's feelings—the poor, the lonely, the sad? Will these actions make you happy?

Show us

God, show us your mercy.

I will listen to God,
and God will give me peace.
If we love God well,
God will always take care of us.

Kindness will walk alongside
telling the truth.

What does the word "fair" mean to you? What do you think this psalm means when it says, "God will always be fair?" Sometimes it is hard to understand the meaning of the word "fair." Sometimes things on Earth don't make a lot of sense. For example: Why do the poor have nowhere to sleep and we have beds? Why do some people who we love leave us? These are hard questions not just for children, but for grown-ups too. What this psalm tells us though is that God knows all, sees all, and he understands what is fair when we cannot. God's mercy and love comforts us during these times. God is always there for us. God is always fair.

your mercy

God will always be fair, and
will give us peace.
Everywhere we look on the
earth, we will see the truth.
When we look up to the
sky, we will know that God
will always be fair.

God will give us everything
we need.
And everything will grow
twice as much!
God will help us to become
friends
with what is right,
and show us the way.

God, show us your mercy.

"Steadfast love and
faithfulness will meet;
righteousness and
peace will kiss each
other. Faithfulness will
spring up from the
ground, and
righteousness will look
down from the sky."
[PSALM 85]

Be with me

God, please be with me
when I am in trouble.

We know God well.
We should all say to God:
"You are my protector, and I trust you."

Evil and sadness will never take over,
for God is in charge of all the angels,
and they will guard and protect us.

"Let the light of your face
shine on us, O LORD."
[PSALM 4]

The angels will keep us safe,
If we trip and fall,
we will be picked up quickly.

God says to us, "All those who
stay close to me,
will only have good things
because they look to me for help.
They will call out and pray to me,
and I will answer their prayers.
When they are sad, I will be with them,
and give them happiness forever."

God, please be with me when I am in trouble.

God is always with us and by our side. In this psalm, we hear that angels will be with us and keep us safe. Have you ever felt that someone is looking out for you and keeping you from harm? Did you ever feel that God or someone was at your side in your life? When you crossed the street? When you were about to fall off your bike? When you were lost and then found your way?

Psalms for when I am calm and filled with faith

You are my

"The LORD is my shepherd, I shall not want." [PSALM 23]

God, you are my Shepherd.

God, you always shepherd me,
and I need nothing more.
The grass you lead me to
is so green, and very peaceful.
You give me cool water
that calms me,
and helps me feel like a new person.

If God is our shepherd, then we are the sheep. We flock together, but sometimes we each break away from the flock and we need the shepherd to bring us back and return us to safety. Like sheep, we need to be led in the right direction or we will get lost. God is our shepherd and will lead the way. All we need to do is follow and trust our shepherd. Where is God, our shepherd, leading you?

62

shepherd

You always guide me,
you come through for me.
If I stumble in the dark,
I will have nothing to fear.
You are there, always strong for me,
you help me feel safe.

You feed me well
in the presence of those
who would want to harm me.
You soothe me with oil,
and my cup is filled to the top.

Goodness and kindness will always be with me,
as long as I am alive.
I will be with God, in God's house.
All the time.

God, you are my Shepherd.

You are

You are my light and you keep me safe.

God, you are my light, and you always
keep me safe.
Why should I ever be afraid?
You always take care of me,
so I should never worry.

What do you think this psalm means when it says that God is "my light?" Does God glow in the dark like your glow-in-the-dark stickers? If we turn off the lights in our rooms, will God appear? Or does the passage mean that God shows us the way, just as light allows us to see in a dark room. Seeing through God makes us see the goodness in the world. Turning on God in our hearts is like turning on the lights in a dark room. Once we flip the switch, we can see everything!

my light

I only want one thing,
God;
I want to live and
be with you, always,
I want to see you.

I know that someday I
will see you
and I will live forever!
I will wait and be brave,
I will wait for you!

You are my light and you
keep me safe.

"The LORD is my light
and my salvation;
whom shall I fear?"
[PSALM 27]

God is the one I turn to

"On God rests my deliverance and my honor; my mighty rock, my refuge is in God."
[PSALM 62]

When I need to rest,
God is the one I turn to.

God is the only one
who can
really help me to rest,
and help me to feel
safe.
God is like a strong,
hard rock,
keeping me steady all
the time.

Everyone should rest in
God,
God is the only one
who gives me hope.

I will sing and be
happy,
I will always rely on
God.
Everyone who has a
broken heart,
should reach out to
God.

When I need to rest,
God is the one I turn to.

God is like a superhero, so we should rest our fears and not worry. God can handle even the toughest case! God is always ready to help us. And, God is surely mightier than any superhero that you could imagine! God is the strongest. God is the fastest. God is the mightiest. God is the best! God has the power to hold the whole world in one hand, and comfort the smallest child with the other. When you need help—you do not need any other superhero, just call upon God!

You alone

You alone,
you alone are peace.

O God, I am not too proud,
nor selfish,
and I try not to be distracted
with things that are great.

Ask a parent or a loved one what you were like when you were a baby. It is fun to recall those memories with the ones who love you most. Ask how you looked when you slept in a loved one's arms. Were you calm and peaceful? Do you have a picture of yourself sleeping as a baby? Have you ever seen a baby asleep in his or her mother's arms? How does that make you feel? Calm? Peaceful? Relaxed? Happy? How wonderful it must be for God to cradle you everyday, from the time you were a baby, now, and for all time! We are all God's children. We are all in God's loving arms—peaceful, safe and calm.

are my peace

I have tried to be
calm and quiet
like a little baby in
its mother's arms.
My soul is the same
way with you.

You alone,
You alone are
peace.

"But I have calmed and
quieted my soul."
[PSALM 131]

You made me a wonderful being

"For it was you who formed my inward parts; you knit me together in my mother's womb. I praise you, for I am fearfully and wonderfully made. Wonderful are your works; that I know very well."

[PSALM 139]

God, you made me a wonderful being,
and I praise and thank you!

You always look deep into my heart,
God,
because you know everything about me.
You know when I sleep,
you know when I am playing,
and you know everything I am thinking.
You know everything I do,
and every place I go.

You alone made me.
You placed me in my mother's womb,
and I praise and thank you for the
wonderful way you created me.

Everything you do is fantastic!
Nothing is hidden from you,
for you know absolutely everything.

God, you made me a wonderful being,
and I praise and thank you!

You are wonderful in so many ways! Only God knows your full potential! Today, think of all the wonderful gifts God has given to you. Get out a piece of paper and start a list. Ask an adult or a loved one to help you name all the gifts, talents and blessings you possess. You can do it with friends or with the entire family too. Together you can share each of your wonderful gifts from God. Keep the list out where you can see it and add to the list everyday. Remember to thank God every time you add a new or special gift to the list! For example, you can write: "Thanks God, for my brown eyes!" Or, "Thanks God, for the gift of sight" Or, "Thanks God, for my mind that helped me read this book!" You have so many gifts and talents, so many things that make you wonderful! Remember them all, and remember to always thank and praise God for each one!